Christopher Columbus
And The New World of His Discovery
Volume 2

FILSON YOUNG

[ZHINGOORA BOOKS]

This edition is published by
Zhingoora Books.

About Author

Alexander Bell Filson Young was a journalist, BBC programme advisor and author. His wrote the book on Titanic, a RMS Titanic ship. His famous works includeTitanic, The Relief of Mafekingand etc.

CHAPTER IX

WANDERINGS WITH AN IDEA

The man to whom Columbus proposed to address his request for means with which to make a voyage of discovery was no less a person than the new King of Portugal. Columbus was never a man of petty or small ideas; if he were going to do a thing at all, he went about it in a large and comprehensive way; and all his life he had a way of going to the fountainhead, and of making flights and leaps where other men would only climb or walk, that had much to do with his ultimate success. King John, moreover, had shown himself thoroughly sympathetic to the spirit of discovery; Columbus, as we have seen, had already been employed in a trusted capacity in one of the royal expeditions; and he rightly thought that, since he had to ask the help of some one in his enterprise, he might as well try to enlist the Crown itself in the service of his great Idea. He was not prepared, however, to go directly to the King and ask for ships; his proposal would have to be put in a way that would appeal to the royal ambition, and would also satisfy the King that there was really a destination in view for the expedition. In other words Columbus had to propose to go somewhere; it would not do to say that he was going west into the Atlantic Ocean to look about him. He therefore devoted all his energies to putting his proposal on what is called a business footing, and expressing his vague, sublime Idea in common and practical terms.

The people who probably helped him most in this were his brother Bartholomew and Martin Behaim, the great authority on scientific navigation, who had been living in Lisbon for some time and with whom Columbus was acquainted. Behaim, who was at this time about forty eight years of age, was born at Nuremberg, and was a pupil of Regiomontanus, the great German astronomer. A very interesting man, this, if we could decipher his features and character; no mere star-gazing visionary, but a man of the world, whose scientific lore was combined with a wide and liberal experience of life. He was not only learned in cosmography and astronomy, but he had a genius for mechanics and made beautiful instruments; he was a merchant also, and combined a little business with his scientific travels. He had been employed at Lisbon in adapting the astrolabe of Regiomontanus for the use of sailors at sea; and in these labours he was assisted by two people who were destined to have a weighty influence on the career of Columbus—Doctors Rodrigo and Joseph, physicians or advisers to the King, and men of great academic reputation. There was nothing known about cosmography or astronomy that Behaim did not know; and he had just come back from an expedition on which he had been despatched, with Rodrigo and Joseph, to take the altitude of the sun in Guinea.

Columbus was not the man to neglect his opportunities, and there can be no doubt that as soon as his purpose had established itself in his mind he made use of every opportunity that presented itself for improving his meagre scientific knowledge, in order that his proposal might be set forth in a plausible form. In other words, he got up the subject. The whole of his geographical reading with regard to the Indies up to this time had been in the travels of Marco Polo; the others—whose works he quoted from so freely in later years were then known to him only by name, if at all. Behaim, however, could tell him a good deal about the supposed circumference of the earth, the extent of the Asiatic continent, and so on. Every new fact that Columbus heard he seized and pressed into the service of his Idea; where there was a choice of facts, or a difference of opinion between scientists, he chose the facts that were most convenient, and the opinions that fitted best with his own beliefs. The very word "Indies" was synonymous with unbounded wealth; there certainly would be riches to tempt the King with; and Columbus, being a religious man, hit also on the happy idea of setting forth the spiritual glory of carrying the light of faith across the Sea of Darkness, and making of the heathen a heritage for the Christian Church. So that, what with one thing and another, he soon had his proposals formally arranged.

Imagine him, then, actually at Court, and having an audience of the King, who could scarcely believe his ears. Here was a man, of whom he knew nothing but that his conduct of a caravel had been well spoken of in the recent expedition to Guinea, actually proposing to sail out west into the Atlantic and to cross the unknown part of the world. Certainly his proposals seemed plausible, but still—. The earth was round, said Columbus, and therefore there was a way from East to West and from West to East. The prophet Esdras, a scientific authority that even His Majesty would hardly venture to doubt, had laid it down that only one-seventh of the earth was covered by waters. From this fact Columbus deduced that the maritime space extending westward between the shores of Europe and eastern coast of Asia could not be large; and by sailing westward he proposed to reach certain lands of which he claimed to have knowledge. The sailors' tales, the logs of driftwood, the dead bodies, were all brought into the proposals; in short, if His Majesty would grant some ships, and consent to making Columbus Admiral over all the islands that he might discover, with full viceregal state, authority, and profit, he would go and discover them.

There are two different accounts of what the King said when this proposal was made to him. According to some authorities, John was impressed by Columbus's proposals, and inclined to provide him with the necessary ships, but he could not assent to all the titles and rewards which Columbus demanded as a price for his services. Barros, the Portuguese historian, on the other hand, represents that the whole idea was too fantastic to be seriously entertained by the King for a moment, and that although he at once made up his mind to refuse the request he preferred to delegate his refusal to a commission. Whatever may be the truth as to King John's opinions, the commission was certainly appointed, and consisted of three persons, to wit: Master Rodrigo, Master Joseph the Jew, and the Right Reverend Cazadilla, Bishop of Ceuta.

Before these three learned men must Columbus now appear, a little less happy in his mind, and wishing that he knew more Latin. Master Rodrigo, Master Joseph the Jew, the Right Reverend Cazadilla: three pairs of cold eyes turned rather haughtily on the Genoese adventurer; three brains much steeped in learning, directed in judgment on the Idea of a man with no learning at all. The Right Reverend Cazadilla, being the King's confessor, and a bishop into the bargain, could speak on that matter of converting the heathen; and he was of opinion that it could not be done. Joseph the Jew, having made voyages, and worked with Behaim at the astrolabe, was surely an authority on navigation; and he was of opinion that it could not be done. Rodrigo, being also a very learned man, had read many books which Columbus had not read; and he was of opinion that it could not be done. Three learned opinions against one Idea; the Idea is bound to go. They would no doubt question Columbus on the scientific aspect of the matter, and would soon discover his grievous lack of academic knowledge. They would quote fluently passages from writers that he had not heard of; if he had not heard of them, they seemed to imply, no wonder he made such foolish proposals. Poor Columbus stands there puzzled, dissatisfied, tongue-tied. He cannot answer these wiseacres in their own learned lingo; what they say, or what they quote, may be true or it may not; but it has nothing to do with his Idea. If he opens his mouth to justify himself, they refute him with arguments that he does not understand; there is a wall between them. More than a wall; there is a world between them! It is his 'credo' against their 'ignoro'; it is, his 'expecto' against their 'non video'. Yet in his 'credo' there lies a power of which they do not dream; and it rings out in a trumpet note across the centuries, saluting the life force that opposes its irresistible "I will" to the feeble "Thou canst not" of the worldly-wise. Thus, in about the year 1483, did three learned men sit in judgment upon our ignorant Christopher. Three learned men: Doctors Rodrigo, Joseph the Jew, and the Right Reverend Cazadilla, Bishop of Ceuta; three risen, stuffed to the eyes and ears with learning; stuffed so full indeed that eyes and ears are closed with it. And three men, it would appear, wholly destitute of mother-wit.

After all his preparations this rebuff must have been a serious blow to Columbus. It was not his only trouble, moreover. During the last year he had been earning nothing; he was already in imagination the Admiral of the Ocean Seas; and in the anticipation of the much higher duties to which he hoped to be devoted it is not likely that he would continue at his humble task of making maps and charts. The result was that he got into debt, and it was absolutely necessary that something should be done. But a darker trouble had also almost certainly come to him about this time. Neither the day nor the year of Philippa's death is known; but it is likely that it occurred soon after Columbus's failure at the Portuguese Court, and immediately before his departure into Spain. That anonymous life, fulfilling itself so obscurely in companionship and motherhood, as softly as it floated upon the page of history, as softly fades from it again. Those kind eyes, that encouraging voice, that helping hand and friendly human soul are with him no longer; and after the interval of peace and restful growth that they afforded Christopher must strike his tent and go forth upon another stage of his pilgrimage with a heavier and sterner heart.

Two things are left to him: his son Diego, now an articulate little creature with character and personality of his own, and with strange, heart-breaking reminiscences of his mother in voice and countenance and manner—that is one possession; the other is his Idea. Two things alive and satisfactory, amid the ruin and loss of other possessions; two reasons for living and prevailing. And these two possessions Columbus took with him when he set out for Spain in the year 1485.

His first care was to take little Diego to the town of Huelva, where there lived a sister of Philippa's who had married a Spaniard named Muliartes. This done, he was able to devote himself solely to the furtherance of his Idea. For this purpose he went to Seville, where he attached himself for a little while to a group of his countrymen who were settled there, among them Antonio and Alessandro Geraldini, and made such momentary living as was possible to him by his old trade. But the Idea would not sleep. He talked of nothing else; and as men do who talk of an idea that possesses them wholly, and springs from the inner light of faith, he interested and impressed many of his hearers. Some of them suggested one thing, some another; but every one was agreed that it would be a good thing if he could enlist the services of the great Count (afterwards Duke) of Medini Celi, who had a palace at Rota, near Cadiz.

This nobleman was one of the most famous of the grandees of Spain, and lived in mighty state upon his territory along the sea-shore, serving the Crown in its wars and expeditions with the power and dignity of an ally rather than of a subject. His domestic establishment was on a princely scale, filled with chamberlains, gentlemenat-arms, knights, retainers, and all the panoply of social dignity; and there was also place in his household for persons of merit and in need of protection. To this great man came Columbus with his Idea. It attracted the Count, who was a judge of men and perhaps of ideas also; and Columbus, finding some hope at last in his attitude, accepted the hospitality offered to him, and remained at Rota through the winter of 1485-86. He had not been very hopeful when he arrived there, and had told the Count that he had thought of going to the King of France and asking for help from him; but the Count, who found something respectable and worthy of consideration in the Idea of a man who thought nothing of a journey in its service from one country to another and one sovereign to another, detained him, and played with the Idea himself. Three or four caravels were nothing to the Count of Medina Eeli; but on the other hand the man was a grandee and a diplomat, with a nice sense of etiquette and of what was due to a reigning house. Either there was nothing in this Idea, in which case his caravels would be employed to no purpose, or there was so much in it that it was an undertaking, not merely for the Count of Medina Celi, but for the Crown of Castile. Lands across the ocean, and untold gold and riches of the Indies, suggested complications with foreign Powers, and transactions with the Pope himself, that would probably be a little too much even for the good Count; therefore with a curious mixture of far-sighted generosity and shrewd security he wrote to Queen Isabella, recommending Columbus to her, and asking her to consider his Idea; asking her also, in case anything should come of it, to remember him (the Count), and to let him have a finger in the pie. Thus, with much literary circumstance and elaboration of politeness, the Count of Medina Celi to Queen Isabella.

Follows an interval of suspense, the beginning of a long discipline of suspense to which Columbus was to be subjected; and presently comes a favourable reply from the Queen, commanding that Columbus should be sent to her. Early in 1486 he set out for Cordova, where the Court was then established, bearing another letter from the Count in which his own private requests were repeated, and perhaps a little emphasised. Columbus was lodged in the house of Alonso de Quintanilla, Treasurer to the Crown of Castile, there to await an audience with Queen Isabella.

While he is waiting, and getting accustomed to his new surroundings, let us consider these two monarchs in whose presence he is soon to appear, and upon whose decision hangs some part of the world's destiny. Isabella first; for in that strange duet of government it is her womanly soprano that rings most clearly down the corridors of Time. We discern in her a very busy woman, living a difficult life with much tact and judgment, and exercising to some purpose that amiable taste for "doing good" that marks the virtuous lady of station in every age. This, however, was a woman who took risks with her eyes open, and steered herself cleverly in perilous situations, and guided others with a firm hand also, and in other ways made good her claim to be a ruler. The consent and the will of her people were her great strength; by them she dethroned her niece and ascended the throne of Castile. She had the misfortune to be at variance with her husband in almost every matter of policy dear to his heart; she opposed the expulsion of the Jews and the establishment of the Inquisition; but when she failed to get her way, she was still able to preserve her affectionate relations with her husband without disagreement and with happiness. If she had a fault it was the common one of being too much under the influence of her confessors; but it was a fault that was rarely allowed to disturb the balance of her judgment. She liked clever people also; surrounded herself with men of letters and of science, fostered all learned institutions, and delighted in the details of civil administration. A very dignified and graceful figure, that could equally adorn a Court drawing-room or a field of battle; for she actually went into the field, and wore armour as becomingly as silk and ermine. Firm, constant, clever, alert, a little given to fussiness perhaps, but sympathetic and charming, with some claims to genius and some approach to grandeur of soul: so much we may say truly of her inner self. Outwardly she was a woman well formed, of medium height, a very dignified and graceful carriage, eyes of a clear summer blue, and the red and gold of autumn in her hair—these last inherited from her English grandmother.

Ferdinand of Aragon appears not quite so favourably in our pages, for he never thought well of Columbus or of his proposals; and when he finally consented to the expedition he did so with only half a heart, and against his judgment. He was an extremely enterprising, extremely subtle, extremely courageous, and according to our modern notions, an extremely dishonest man; that is to say, his standards of honour were not those which we can accept nowadays. He thought nothing of going back on a promise, provided he got a priestly dispensation to do so; he juggled with his cabinets, and stopped at nothing in order to get his way; he had a craving ambition, and was lacking in magnanimity; he loved dominion, and cared very little for glory. A very capable man; so capable that in spite of his defects he was regarded by his subjects as wise and prudent; so capable that he used his weaknesses of character to strengthen and further the purposes of his reign. A very cold man also, quick and sure in his judgments, of wide understanding and grasp of affairs; simple and austere in dress and diet, as austerity was counted in that period of splendour; extremely industrious, and close in his observations and judgments of men. To the bodily eye he appeared as a man of middle size, sturdy and athletic, face burned a brick red with exposure to the sun and open air; hair and eyebrows of a bright chestnut; a well-formed and not unkindly mouth; a voice sharp and unmelodious, issuing in quick fluent speech. This was the man that earned from the Pope, for himself and his successors, the title of "Most Catholic Majesty."

The Queen was very busy indeed with military preparations; but in the midst of her interviews with nobles and officers, contractors and state officials, she snatched a moment to receive the person Christopher Columbus. With that extreme mental agility which is characteristic of busy sovereigns all the force of this clever woman's mind was turned for a moment on Christopher, whose Idea had by this time invested him with a dignity which no amount of regal state could abash. There was very little time. The Queen heard what Columbus had to say, cutting him short, it is likely, with kindly tact, and suppressing his tendency to launch out into long-winded speeches. What she saw she liked; and, being too busy to give to this proposal the attention that it obviously merited, she told Columbus that the matter would be fully gone into and that in the meantime he must regard himself as the guest of the Court. And so, in the countenance of a smile and a promise, Columbus bows himself out. For the present he must wait a little and his hot heart must contain itself while other affairs, looming infinitely larger than his Idea on the royal horizon, receive the attention of the Court.

It was not the happiest moment, indeed, in which to talk of ships and charts, and lonely sea-roads, and faraway undiscovered shores. Things at home were very real and lively in those spring days at Cordova. The war against the Moors had reached a critical stage; King Ferdinand was away laying siege to the city of Loxa, and though the Queen was at Cordova she was entirely occupied with the business of collecting and forwarding troops and supplies to his aid. The streets were full of soldiers; nobles and grandees from all over the country were arriving daily with their retinues; glitter and splendour, and the pomp of warlike preparation, filled the city. Early in June the Queen herself went to the front and joined her husband in the siege of Moclin; and when this was victoriously ended, and they had returned in triumph to Cordova, they had to set out again for Gallicia to suppress a rebellion there. When that was over they did not come back to Cordova at all, but repaired at once to Salamanca to spend the winter there.

At the house of Alonso de Quintanilla, however, Columbus was not altogether wasting his time. He met there some of the great persons of the Court, among them the celebrated Pedro Gonzalez de Mendoza, Archbishop of Toledo and Grand Cardinal of Spain. This was far too great a man to be at this time anything like a friend of Columbus; but Columbus had been presented to him; the Cardinal would know his name, and what his business was; and that is always a step towards consideration. Cabrero, the royal Chamberlain, was also often a fellow-guest at the

Treasurer's table; and with him Columbus contracted something like a friendship. Every one who met him liked him; his dignity, his simplicity of thought and manner, his experience of the sea, and his calm certainty and conviction about the stupendous thing which he proposed to do, could not fail to attract the liking and admiration of those with whom he came in contact. In the meantime a committee appointed by the Queen sat upon his proposals. The committee met under the presidentship of Hernando de Talavera, the prior of the monastery of Santa Maria del Prado, near Valladolid, a pious ecclesiastic, who had the rare quality of honesty, and who was therefore a favourite with Queen Isabella; she afterwards created him Archbishop of Granada. He was not, however, poor honest soul! quite the man to grasp and grapple with this wild scheme for a voyage across the ocean. Once more Columbus, as in Portugal, set forth his views with eloquence and conviction; and once more, at the tribunal of learning, his unlearned proposals were examined and condemned. Not only was Columbus's Idea regarded as scientifically impossible, but it was also held to come perilously near to heresy, in its assumption of a state of affairs that was clearly at variance with the writings of the Fathers and the sacred Scriptures themselves.

This new disappointment, bitter though it was, did not find Columbus in such friendless and unhappy circumstances as those in which he left Portugal. He had important friends now, who were willing and anxious to help him, and among them was one to whom he turned, in his profound depression, for religious and friendly consolation. This was Diego de DEA, prior of the Dominican convent of San Estevan at Salamanca, who was also professor of theology in the university there and tutor to the young Prince Juan. Of all those who came in contact with Columbus at this time this man seems to have understood him best, and to have realised where his difficulty lay. Like many others who are consumed with a burning idea Columbus was very probably at this time in danger of becoming possessed with it like a monomaniac; and his new friends saw that if he were to make any impression upon the conservative learning of the time to which a decision in such matters was always referred he must have some opportunity for friendly discussion with learned men who were not inimical to him, and who were not in the position of judges examining a man arraigned before them and pleading for benefits.

When the Court went to Salamanca at the end of 1486, DEA arranged that Columbus should go there too, and he lodged him in a country farm called Valcuebo, which belonged to his convent and was equi-distant from it and the city. Here the good Dominican fathers came and visited him, bringing with them professors from the university, who discussed patiently with Columbus his theories and ambitions, and, himself all conscious, communicated new knowledge to him, and quietly put him right on many a scientific point. There were professors of cosmography and astronomy in the university, familiar with the works of Alfraganus and Regiomontanus. It is likely that it was at this time that Columbus became possessed of d'Ailly's 'Imago Mundi', which little volume contained a popular resume of the scientific views of Strabo, Pliny, Ptolemy, and others, and was from this time forth Columbus's constant companion.

Here at Valcuebo and later, when winter came, in the great hall of the Dominican convent at Salamanca, known as the "De Profundis" hall, where the monks received guests and held discussions, the Idea of Columbus was ventilated and examined. He heard what friendly sceptics had to say about it; he saw the kind of argument that he would have to oppose to the existing scientific and philosophical knowledge on cosmography. There is no doubt that he learnt a good deal at this time; and more important even than this, he got his project known and talked about; and he made powerful friends, who were afterwards to be of great use to him. The Marquesa de Moya, wife of his friend Cabrera, took a great liking to him; and as she was one of the oldest and closest friends of the Queen, it is likely that she spoke many a good word for Columbus in Isabella's ear.

By the time the Court moved to Cordova early in 1487, Columbus was once more hopeful of getting a favourable hearing. He followed the Court to Cordova, where he received a gracious message from the Queen to the effect that she had not forgotten him, and that as soon as her military preoccupations permitted it, she would go once more, and more fully, into his proposals. In the meantime he was attached to the Court, and received a quarterly payment of 3000 maravedis. It seemed as though the unfavourable decision of Talavera's committee had been forgotten.

In the meantime he was to have a change of scene. Isabella followed Ferdinand to the siege of Malaga, where the Court was established; and as there were intervals in which other than military business might be transacted, Columbus was ordered to follow them in case his affairs should come up for consideration. They did not; but the man himself had an experience that may have helped to keep his thoughts from brooding too much on his unfulfilled ambition. Years afterwards, when far away on lonely seas, amid the squalor of a little ship and the staggering buffets of a gale, there would surely sometimes leap into his memory a brightly coloured picture of this scene in the fertile valley of Malaga: the silken pavilions of the Court, the great encampment of nobility with its arms and banners extending in a semicircle to the seashore, all glistening and moving in the bright sunshine. There was added excitement at this time at an attempt to assassinate Ferdinand and Isabella, a fanatic Moor having crept up to one of the pavilions and aimed a blow at two people whom he mistook for the King and Queen. They turned out to be Don Alvaro de Portugal, who was dangerously wounded, and Columbus's friend, the Marquesa de Moya, who was unhurt; but it was felt that the King and Queen had had a narrow escape. The siege was raised on the 18th of August, and the sovereigns went to spend the winter at Zaragoza; and Columbus, once more condemned to wait, went back to Cordova.

It was here that he contracted his second and, so far as we know, his last romantic attachment. The long idle days of summer and autumn at Cordova, empty of all serious occupation, gave nature an opportunity for indulging her passion for life and continuity. Among Christopher's friends at Cordova was the family of Arana, friendly hospitable souls, by some accounts noble and by others not noble, and certainly in somewhat poor circumstances, who had welcomed him to their house, listened to his plans with enthusiasm, and formed a life-long friendship with him. Three members of this family are known to us—two brothers, Diego and Pedro, both of whom commanded ships in Columbus's expeditions, and a sister Beatriz. Columbus was now a man of six-and-thirty, while she was little more than a girl; he was handsome and winning, distinguished by the daring and importance of his scheme, full of thrilling and romantic talk of distant lands; a very interesting companion, we may be sure. No wonder she fell in love with Christopher; no wonder that he, feeling lonely and depressed by the many postponements of his suit at Court, and in need of sympathy and encouragement, fell in these blank summer days into an intimacy that flamed into a brief but happy passion. Why Columbus never married Beatriz de Arana we cannot be sure, for it is almost certain that his first wife had died some time before. Perhaps he feared to involve himself in any new or embarrassing ties; perhaps he loved unwillingly, and against his reason; perhaps—although the suggestion is not a happy one—he by this time did not think poor Beatriz good enough for the Admiral-elect of the Ocean Seas; perhaps (and more probably) Beatriz was already married and deserted, for she bore the surname of Enriquez; and in that case, there being no such thing as a divorce in the Catholic Church, she must either sin or be celibate. But however that may be, there was an uncanonical alliance between them which evidently did not in the least scandalise her brothers and which resulted in the birth of Ferdinand Columbus in the following year. Christopher, so communicative and discursive upon some of his affairs, is as reticent about Beatriz as he was about Philippa. Beatriz shares with his legitimate wife the curious distinction of being spoken of by Columbus to posterity only in his will, which was executed at Valladolid the day before he died. In the dry ink and vellum of that ancient legal document is his only record of these two passions. The reference to Beatriz is as follows:

"And I direct him [Diego] to make provision for Beatriz Enriquez, mother of D. Fernando, my son, that she may be able to live honestly, being a person to whom I am under very great obligation. And this shall be done for the satisfaction of my conscience, because this matter weighs heavily upon my soul. The reason for which it is not fitting to write here."

About the condition of Beatriz, temporal and spiritual, there has been much controversy; but where the facts are all so buried and inaccessible it is unseemly to agitate a veil which we cannot lift, and behind which Columbus himself sheltered this incident of his life. "Acquainted with poverty" is one fragment of fact concerning her that has come down to us; acquainted also with love and with happiness, it would seem, as many poor persons undoubtedly are. Enough for us to know that in the city of Cordova there lived a woman, rich or poor, gentle or humble, married or not married, who brought for a time love and friendly companionship into the life of Columbus; that she gave what she had for giving, without stint or reserve, and that she became the mother of a son who inherited much of what was best in his father, and but for whom the world would be in even greater darkness than it is on the subject of Christopher himself. And so no more of Beatriz Enriquez de Arana, whom "God has in his keeping"—and has had now these many centuries of Time.

Thus passed the summer and autumn of 1487; precious months, precious years slipping by, and the great purpose as yet unfulfilled and seemingly no nearer to fulfilment. It is likely that Columbus kept up his applications to the Court, and received polite and delaying replies. The next year came, and the Court migrated from Zaragoza to Murcia, from Murcia to Valladolid, from Valladolid to Medina del Campo. Columbus attended it in one or other of these places, but without result. In August Beatriz gave birth to a son, who was christened Ferdinand, and who lived to be a great comfort to his father, if not to her also. But the miracle of paternity was not now so new and wonderful as it had been; the battle of life, with its crosses and difficulties, was thick about him; and perhaps he looked into this new-comer's small face with conflicting thoughts, and memories of the long white beach and the crashing surf at Porto Santo, and regret for things lost—so strangely mingled and inconsistent are the threads of human thought. At last he decided to turn his face elsewhere. In September 1488 he went to Lisbon, for what purpose it is not certain; possibly in connection with the affairs of his dead wife; and probably also in the expectation of seeing his brother Bartholomew, to whom we may now turn our attention for a moment.

After the failure of Columbus's proposals to the King of Portugal in 1486, and the break-up of his home there, Bartholomew had also left Lisbon. Bartholomew Diaz, a famous Portuguese navigator, was leaving for the African coast in August, and Bartholomew Columbus is said to have joined his small expedition of three caravels. As they neared the latitude of the Cape which he was trying to make, he ran into a gale which drove him a long way out of his course, west and south.

The wind veered round from north-east to north-west, and he did not strike the land again until May 1487. When he did so his crew insisted upon his returning, as they declined to go any further south. He therefore turned to the west, and then made the startling discovery that in the course of the tempest he had been blown round the Cape, and that the land he had made was to the eastward of it; and he therefore rounded it on his way home. He arrived back in Lisbon in December 1488, when Columbus met his brother again, and was present at the reception of Diaz by the King of Portugal. They had a great deal to tell each other, these two brothers; in the two years and a half that had gone since they had parted a great deal had happened to them; and they both knew a good deal more about the great question in which they, were interested than they had known when last they talked.

It is to this period that I attribute the inception, if not the execution, of the forgery of the Toscanelli correspondence, if, as I believe, it was a forgery. Christopher's unpleasant experiences before learned committees and commissions had convinced him that unless he were armed with some authoritative and documentary support for his theories they had little chance of acceptance by the learned. The, Idea was right; he knew that; but before he could convince the academic mind, he felt that it must have the imprimatur of a mind whose learning could not be impugned. Therefore it is not an unfair guess—and it can be nothing more than a guess—that Christopher and Bartholomew at this point laid their heads together, and decided that the next time Christopher had to appear before a commission he would, so to speak, have something "up his sleeve." It was a risky thing to do, and must in any case be used only as a very last resource; which would account for the fact that the Toscanelli correspondence was never used at all, and is not mentioned in any document known to men written until long after Columbus's death.

But these summers and winters of suspense are at last drawing to a close, and we must follow Christopher rapidly through them until the hour of his triumph. He was back in Spain in the spring of 1489, his travelling expenses being defrayed out of the royal purse; and a little later he was once more amid scenes of war at the siege of Baza, and, if report is true, taking a hand himself, not without distinction. It was there that he saw the two friars from the convent of the Holy Sepulchre at Jerusalem, who brought a message from the Grand Soldan of Egypt, threatening the destruction of the Sepulchre if the Spanish sovereigns did not desist from the war against Granada; and it was there that in his simple and pious mind he formed the resolve that if ever his efforts should be crowned with success, and he himself become rich and powerful, he would send a crusade for the rescue of the Holy Sepulchre. And it was there that, on the 22nd of December, he saw Boabdil, the elder of the two rival Kings of Granada, surrender all his rights and claims to Spain. Surely now there will be a chance for him? No; there is another interruption, this time occasioned by the royal preparations for the marriage of the Princess Isabella to the heir of Portugal. Poor Columbus, sickened and disappointed by these continual delays, irritated by a sense of the waste of his precious time, follows the Court about from one place to another, raising a smile here and a scoff there, and pointed at by children in the street. There, is nothing so ludicrous as an Idea to those who do not share it.

Another summer, another winter, lost out of a life made up of a limited number of summers and winters; a few more winters and summers, thinks Christopher, and I shall be in a world where Ideas are not needed, and where there is nothing left to discover! Something had to be done. In the beginning of 1491 there was only one thing spoken of at Court—the preparations for the siege of Granada, which did not interest Columbus at all. The camp of King Ferdinand was situated at Santa Fe, a few miles to the westward of Granada, and Columbus came here late in the year, determined to get a final answer one way or the other to his question. He made his application, and the busy monarchs once more adopted their usual polite tactics. They appointed a junta, which was presided over by no less a person than the Cardinal of Spain, Gonzales de Mendoza: Once more the weary business was gone through, but Columbus must have had some hopes of success, since he did not produce his forged Toscanelli correspondence. It was no scruple of conscience that held him back, we may be sure; the crafty Genoese knew nothing about such scruples in the attainment of a great object; he would not have hesitated to adopt any means to secure an end which he felt to be so desirable. So it is probable that either he was not quite sure of his ground and his courage failed him, or that he had hopes, owing to his friendship with so many of the members of the junta, that a favourable decision would at last be arrived at. In this he was mistaken. The Spanish prelates again quoted the Fathers of the Church, and disposed of his proposals simply on the ground that they were heretical. Much talk, and much wagging of learned heads; and still no mother-wit or gleam of light on this obscurity of learning. The junta decided against the proposals, and reported its decision to the King and Queen. The monarchs, true to their somewhat hedging methods when there was anything to be gained by hedging, informed Columbus that at present they were too much occupied with the war to grant his requests; but that, when the preoccupations and expenses of the campaign were a thing of the past, they might again turn their attention to his very interesting suggestion.

It was at this point that the patience of Columbus broke down. Too many promises had been made to him, and hope had been held out to him too often for him to believe any more in it. Spain, he decided, was useless; he would try France; at least he would be no worse off there. But he had first of all to settle his affairs as well as possible. Diego, now a growing boy nearly eleven years old, had been staying with Beatriz at Cordova, and going to school there; Christopher would take him back to his aunt's at Huelva before he went away. He set out with a heavy heart, but with purpose and determination unimpaired.

CHAPTER X

OUR LADY OF LA RABIDA

It is a long road from Santa Fe to Huelva, a long journey to make on foot, and the company of a sad heart and a little talking boy, prone to sudden weariness and the asking of innumerable difficult questions, would not make it very much shorter. Every step that Christopher took carried him farther away from the glittering scene where his hopes had once been so bright, and were now fallen to the dust; and every step brought him nearer that unknown destiny as to which he was in great darkness of mind, and certain only that there was some small next thing constantly to be done: the putting down of one foot after another, the request for food and lodging at the end of each short day's march, the setting out again in the morning. That walk from Santa Fe, so real and painful and wearisome and long a thing to Christopher and Diego, is utterly blank and obliterated for us. What he thought and felt and suffered are things quite dead; what he did-namely, to go and do the immediate thing that it seemed possible and right for him to do—is a living fact to-day, for it brought him, as all brave and honest doing will, a little nearer to his destiny, a little nearer to the truthful realisation of what was in him.

At about a day's journey from Huelva, where the general slope of the land begins to fall towards the sea, two small rivers, the Odiel and the Tinto, which have hitherto been making music each for itself through the pleasant valleys and vineyards of Andalusia, join forces, and run with a deeper stream towards the sea at Palos. The town of Palos lay on the banks of the river; a little to the south of it, and on the brow of a rocky promontory dark with pine trees, there stood the convent of Our Lady of La Rabida. Stood, on this November evening in the year 1491; had stood in some form or other, and used for varying purposes, for many years and centuries before that, even to the time of the Romans; and still stands, a silent and neglected place, yet to be visited and seen by such as are curious. To the door of this place comes Christopher as darkness falls, urged thereto by the plight of Diego, who is tired and hungry. Christopher rings the bell, and asks the porter for a little bread and water for the child, and a lodging for them both. There is some talk at the door; the Franciscan lay brother being given, at all times in the history of his order, to the pleasant indulgence of gossiping conversation, when that is lawful; and the presence of a stranger, who speaks with a foreign accent, being at all times a incident of interest and even of excitement in the quiet life of a monastery. The moment is one big with import to the human race; it marks a period in the history of our man; the scene is worth calling up. Dark night, with sea breezes moaning in the pine trees, outside;

raying light from within falling on the lay brother leaning in the doorway and on the two figures standing without: on Christopher, grave, subdued, weary, yet now as always of pleasant and impressive address, and on the small boy who stands beside him round-eyed and expectant, his fatigue for the moment forgotten in curiosity and anticipation.

While they are talking comes no less a person than the Prior of the monastery, Friar Juan Perez, bustling round, good-natured busybody that he is, to see what is all this talk at the door. The Prior, as is the habit of monks, begins by asking questions. What is the stranger's name? Where does he come from? Where is he going to? What is his business? Is the little boy his son? He has actually come from Santa Fe? The Prior, loving talk after the manner of his kind, sees in this grave and smooth-spoken stranger rich possibilities of talk; possibilities that cannot possibly be exhausted to-night, it being now hard on the hour of Compline; the stranger must come in and rest for tonight at least, and possibly for several nights. There is much bustle and preparation; the travellers are welcomed with monkish hospitality; Christopher, we may be sure, goes and hears the convent singing Compline, and offers up devout prayers for a quiet night and for safe conduct through this vale of tears; and goes thankfully to bed with the plainsong echoing in his ears, and some stoic sense that all days, however hard, have an evening, and all journeys an end.

Next morning the talk begins in earnest, and Christopher, never a very reserved man, finds in the friendly curiosity of the monks abundant encouragement to talk; and before very long he is in full swing with his oft-told story. The Prior is delighted with it; he has not heard anything so interesting for a long time. Moreover, he has not always been in a convent; he was not so long ago confessor to Queen Isabella herself, and has much to communicate and ask concerning that lady. Columbus's proposal does not strike him as being unreasonable at all; but he has a friend in Palos, a very learned man indeed, Doctor Garcia Hernandez, who often comes and has a talk with him; he knows all about astronomy and cosmography; the Prior will send for him. And meanwhile there must be no word of Columbus's departure for a few days at any rate.

Presently Doctor Garcia Hernandez arrives, and the whole story is gone over again. They go at it hammer and tongs, arguments and counter-arguments, reasons for and against, encouragements, and objections. The result is that Doctor Garcia Hernandez, whose learning seems not yet quite to have blinded or deafened him, thinks well of the scheme; thinks so well of it that he protests it will be a thousand pities if the chance of carrying it out is lost to Spain. The worthy Prior, who has been somewhat out of it while the talk about degrees and latitudes has been going on, here strikes in again; he will use his influence. Perhaps the good man, living up here among the pine trees and the sea winds, and involved in the monotonous round of Prime, Lauds, Nones, Vespers, has a regretful thought or two of the time when he moved in the splendid intricacy of Court life; at any rate he is not sorry to have an opportunity of recalling himself to the attention of Her Majesty, for the spiritual safety of whose soul he was once responsible; perhaps, being (in spite of his Nones and Vespers) a human soul, he is glad of an opportunity of opposing the counsels of his successor, Talavera. In a word, he will use his Influence. Then follow much drafting of letters, and laying of heads together, and clatter of monkish tongues; the upshot of which is that a letter is written in which Perez urges his daughter in the Lord in the strongest possible terms not to let slip so glorious an opportunity, not only of fame and increment to her kingdom, but of service to the Church and the kingdom of Heaven itself. He assures her that Columbus is indeed about to depart from the country, but that he (Perez) will detain him at La Rabida until he has an answer from the Queen.

A messenger to carry the letter was found in the person of Sebastian Rodriguez, a pilot of the port, who immediately set off to Santa Fe. It is not likely that Columbus, after so many rebuffs, was very hopeful; but in the meantime, here he was amid the pious surroundings in which the religious part of him delighted, and in a haven of rest after all his turmoils and trials. He could look out to sea over the flecked waters of that Atlantic whose secrets he longed to discover; or he could look down into the busy little port of Palos, and watch the ships sailing in and out across the bar of Saltes. He could let his soul, much battered and torn of late by trials and disappointments, rest for a time on the rock of religion; he could snuff the incense in the chapel to his heart's content, and mingle his rough top-gallant voice with the harsh croak of the monks in the daily cycle of prayer and praise. He could walk with Diego through the sandy roads beneath the pine trees, or through the fields and vineyards below; and above all he could talk to the company that good Perez invited to meet him—among them merchants and sailors from Palos, of whom the chief was Martin Alonso Pinzon, a wealthy landowner and navigator, whose family lived then at Palos, owning the vineyards round about, and whose descendants live there to this day. Pinzon was a listener after Columbus's own heart; he not only believed in his project, but offered to assist it with money, and even to accompany the expedition himself. Altogether a happy and peaceful time, in which hopes revived, and the inner light that, although it had now and then flickered, had never gone out, burned up again in a bright and steady flame.

At the end of a fortnight, and much sooner than had been expected, the worthy pilot returned with a letter from the Queen. Eager hands seized it and opened it; delight beamed from the eyes of the good Prior. The Queen was most cordial to him, thanked him for his intervention, was ready to listen to him and even to be convinced by him; and in the meantime commanded his immediate appearance at the Court, asking that Columbus would be so good as to wait at La Rabida until he should hear further from her. Then followed such a fussing and fuming, such a running hither and thither, and giving and taking of instructions and clatter of tongues as even the convent of La Rabida had probably never known. Nothing will serve the good old busybody, although it is now near midnight, but that he must depart at once. He will not wait for daylight; he will not, the good honest soul! wait at all. He must be off at once; he must have this, he must have that; he will take this, he will leave that behind; or no, he will take that, and leave this behind. He must have a mule, for his old feet will not bear him fast enough; ex-confessors of Her Majesty, moreover, do not travel on foot; and after more fussing and running hither and thither a mule is borrowed from one Juan Rodriguez Cabezudo of Moguer; and with a God-speed from the group standing round the lighted doorway, the old monk sets forth into the night.

It is a strange thing to consider what unimportant flotsam sometimes floats visibly upon the stream of history, while the gravest events are sunk deep beneath its flood. We would give a king's ransom to know events that must have taken place in any one of twenty years in the life of Columbus, but there is no sign of them on the surface of the stream, nor will any fishing bring them to light. Yet here, bobbing up like a cork, comes the name of Juan Rodriguez Cabezudo of Moguer, doubtless a good worthy soul, but, since he has been dead these four centuries and more, of no interest or importance to any human being; yet of whose life one trivial act, surviving the flood of time which has engulfed all else that he thought important, falls here to be recorded: that he did, towards midnight of a day late in December 1491 lend a mule to Friar Juan Perez.

Of that heroic mule journey we have no record; but it brought results enough to compensate the good Prior for all his aching bones and rheumatic joints. He was welcomed by the Queen, who had never quite lost her belief in Columbus, but who had hitherto deferred to the apathy of Ferdinand and the disapproval—of her learned advisers. Now, however, the matter was reopened. She, who sometimes listened to priests with results other than good, heard this worthy priest to good purpose. The feminine friends of Columbus who remembered him at Court also spoke up for him, among them the Marquesa de Moya, with whom he had always been a favourite; and it was decided that his request should be granted and three vessels equipped for the expedition, "that he might go and make discoveries and prove true the words he had spoken."—Moreover, the machinery that had been so hard to move before, turned swiftly now. Diego Prieto, one of the magistrates of Palos, was sent to Columbus at La Rabida, bearing 20,000 maravedis with which he was to buy a mule and decent clothing for himself, and repair immediately to the Court at Santa Fe. Old Perez was in high feather, and busy with his pen. He wrote to Doctor Garcia Hernandez, and also to Columbus, in whose letter the following pleasant passage occurs:

"Our Lord has listened to the prayers of His servant. The wise and virtuous Isabella, touched by the grace of Heaven, gave a favourable hearing to the words of this poor monk. All has turned out well. Far from despising your project, she has adopted it from this time, and she has summoned you to Court to propose the means which seem best to you for the execution of the designs of Providence. My heart swims in a sea of comfort, and my spirit leaps with joy in the Lord. Start at once, for the Queen waits for you, and I much more than she. Commend me to the prayers of my brethren, and of your little Diego. The grace of God be with you, and may Our Lady of La Rabida accompany you."

The news of that day must have come upon Columbus like a burst of sunshine after rain. I like to think how bright must have seemed to him the broad view of land and sea, how deeply the solemn words of the last office which he attended must have sunk into his soul, how great and glad a thing life must have been to him, and how lightly the miles must have passed beneath the feet of his mule as he jogged out on the long road to Santa Fe.

CHAPTER XI

THE CONSENT OF SPAIN

Once more; in the last days of the year 1491, Columbus rode into the brilliant camp which he had quitted a few weeks before with so heavy a heart. Things were changed now. Instead of being a suitor, making a nuisance of himself, and forcing his affairs on the attention of unwilling officials, he was now an invited and honoured guest; much more than that, he was in the position of one who believed that he had a great service to render to the Crown, and who was at last to be permitted to render it.

Even now, at the eleventh hour, there was one more brief interruption. On the 1st of January 1492 the last of the Moorish kings sent in his surrender to King Ferdinand, whom he invited to come and take possession of the city of Granada; and on the next day the Spanish army marched into that city, where, in front of the Alhambra, King Ferdinand received the keys of the castle and the homage of the Moorish king. The wars of eight centuries were at an end, and the Christian banner of Spain floated at last over the whole land. Victory and success were in the air, and the humble Genoese adventurer was to have his share in them. Negotiations of a practical nature were now begun; old friends—Talavera, Luis de Santangel, and the Grand Cardinal himself—were all brought into consultation with the result that matters soon got to the documentary stage. Here, however, there was a slight hitch. It was not simply a matter of granting two, or three ships. The Genoese was making a bargain, and asking an impossible price. Even the great grandees and Court officials, accustomed to the glitter and dignity of titles, rubbed their eyes with astonishment, when they saw what Columbus was demanding. He who had been suing for privileges was now making conditions. And what conditions! He must be created Admiral of all the Ocean Seas and of the new lands, with equal privileges and prerogatives as those appertaining to the High Admiral of Castile, the supreme naval officer of Spain. Not content with sea dignities, he was also to be Viceroy and Governor-General in all islands or mainlands that he might acquire; he wanted a tenth part of the profits resulting from his discoveries, in perpetuity; and he must have the permanent right of contributing an eighth part of the cost of the equipment and have an additional eighth part of the profits; and all his heirs and descendants for ever were to have the same privileges. These conditions were on such a scale as no sovereign could readily approve. Columbus's lack of pedigree, and the fact also that he was a foreigner, made them seem the more preposterous; for although he might receive kindness and even friendship from some of the grand Spaniards with whom he associated, that friendship and kindness were given condescendingly and with a smile. He was delightful when he was merely proposing as a mariner to confer additional grandeur and glory on the Crown; but when it came to demanding titles and privileges which would make him rank with the highest grandees in, the land, the matter took on quite a different colour. It was nonsense; it could not be allowed; and many were the friendly hints that Columbus doubtless received at this time to relinquish his wild demands and not to overreach himself.

But to the surprise and dismay of his friends, who really wished him to have a chance of distinguishing himself, and were shocked at the impediments he was now putting in his own way, the man from Genoa stood firm. What he proposed to do, he said, was worthy of the rewards that he asked; they were due to the importance and grandeur of his scheme, and so on. Nor did he fail to point out that the bestowal of them was a matter altogether contingent on results; if there were no results, there would be no rewards; if there were results, they would be worthy of the rewards. This action of Columbus's deserves close study. He had come to a turning-point in his life. He had been asking, asking, asking, for six years; he had been put off and refused over and over again; people were beginning to laugh at him for a madman; and now, when a combination of lucky chances had brought him to the very door of success, he stood outside the threshold bargaining for a preposterous price before he would come in. It seemed like the densest stupidity. What is the explanation of it?

The only explanation of it is to be found in the character of Columbus. We must try to see him as he is in this forty-second year of his life, bargaining with notaries, bishops, and treasurers; we must try to see where these forty years have brought him, and what they have made of him. Remember the little boy that played in the Vico Dritto di Ponticello, acquainted with poverty, but with a soul in him that could rise beyond it and acquire something of the dignity of that Genoa, arrogant, splendid and devout, which surrounded him during his early years. Remember his long life of obscurity at sea, and the slow kindling of the light of faith in something beyond the familiar horizons; remember the social inequality of his marriage, his long struggle with poverty, his long familiarity with the position of one who asked and did not receive; the many rebuffs and indignities which his Ligurian pride must have received at the hands of all those Spanish dignitaries and grandees—remember all this, and then you will perhaps not wonder so much that Columbus, who was beginning to believe himself appointed by Heaven to this task of discovery, felt that he had much to pay himself back for. One must recognise him frankly for what he was, and for no conventional hero of romance; a man who would reconcile his conscience with anything, and would stop at nothing in the furtherance of what he deemed a good object; and a man at the same time who had a conscience to reconcile, and would, whenever it was necessary, laboriously and elaborately perform the act of reconciliation. When he made these huge demands in Granada he was gambling with his chances; but he was a calculating gambler, just about as cunning and crafty in the weighing of one chance against another as a gambler with a conscience can be; and he evidently realised that his own valuation of the services he proposed to render would not be without its influence on his sovereign's estimate of them. At any rate he was justified by the results, for on the 17th of April 1492, after a deal of talk and bargaining, but apparently without any yielding on Columbus's part, articles of capitulation were drawn up in which the following provisions were made:—

First, that Columbus and his heirs for ever should have the title and office of Admiral in all the islands and continents of the ocean that he or they might discover, with similar honours and prerogatives to those enjoyed by the High Admiral of Castile.

Second, that he and his heirs should be Viceroys and Governors-General over all the said lands and continents, with the right of nominating three candidates for the governing of each island or province, one of whom should be appointed by the Crown.

Third, that he end his heirs should be entitled to one-tenth of all precious stones, metals, spices, and other merchandises, however acquired, within his Admiralty, the cost of acquisition being first deducted.

Fourth, that he or his lieutenants in their districts, and the High Admiral of Castile in his district, should be the sole judge in all disputes arising out of traffic between Spain and the new countries.

Fifth, that he now, and he and his heirs at all times, should have the right to contribute the eighth part of the expense of fitting out expeditions, and receive the eighth part of the profits.

In addition to these articles there was another document drawn up on the 30th of April, which after an infinite preamble about the nature of the Holy Trinity, of the Apostle Saint James, and of the Saints of God generally in their relations to Princes, and with a splendid trailing of gorgeous Spanish names and titles across the page, confers upon our hitherto humble Christopher the right to call himself "Don," and finally raises him, in his own estimation at any rate, to a social level with his proud Spanish friends. It is probably from this time that he adopted the Spanish form of his name, Christoval Colon; but in this narrative I shall retain the more universal form in which it has become familiar to the English-speaking world.

He was now upon a Pisgah height, from which in imagination he could look forth and see his Land of Promise. We also may climb up with him, and stand beside him as he looks westward. We shall not see so clearly as he sees, for we have not his inner light; and it is probable that even he does not see the road at all, but only the goal, a single point of light shining across a gulf of darkness. But from Pisgah there is a view backward as well as forward, and, we may look back for a moment on this last period of Christopher's life in Spain, inwardly to him so full of trouble and difficulty and disappointment, outwardly so brave and glittering, musical with high-sounding names and the clash of arms; gay with sun and shine and colour. The brilliant Court moving from camp to camp with its gorgeous retinues and silken pavilions and uniforms and dresses and armours; the excitement of war, the intrigues of the antechamber—these are the bright fabric of the latter years; and against it, as against a background, stand out the beautiful names of the Spanish associates of Columbus at this time—Medina Celi, Alonso de Quintanilla, Cabrero, Arana, DEA, Hernando de Talavera, Gonzales de Mendoza, Alonso de Cardenas, Perez, Hernandez, Luis de Santangel, and Rodriguez de Maldonado—names that now, in his hour of triumph, are like banners streaming in the wind against a summer sky.

CHAPTER XII

THE PREPARATIONS AT PALOS

The Palos that witnessed the fitting out of the ships of Columbus exists no longer. The soul is gone from it; the trade that in those days made it great and busy has floated away from it into other channels; and it has dwindled and shrunk, until to-day it consists of nothing but a double street of poor white houses, such almost as you may see in any sea-coast village in Ireland. The slow salt tides of the Atlantic come flooding in over the Manto bank, across the bar of Saltes, and, dividing at the tongue of land that separates the two rivers, creep up the mud banks of the Tinto and the Odiel until they lie deep beside the wharves of Huelva and Palos; but although Huelva still has a trade the tides bring nothing to Palos, and take nothing away with them again. From La Rabida now you can no longer see, as Columbus saw, fleets of caravels lying-to and standing off and on outside the bar waiting for the flood tide; only a few poor boats fishing for tunny in the empty sunny waters, or the smoke of a steamer standing on her course for the Guadalquiver or Cadiz.

But in those spring days of 1492 there was a great stir and bustle of preparation in Palos. As soon as the legal documents had been signed Columbus returned there and, taking up his quarters at La Rabida, set about fitting out his expedition. The reason Palos was chosen was an economical one. The port, for some misdemeanour, had lately been condemned to provide two caravels for the service of the Crown for a period of twelve months; and in the impoverished state of the royal exchequer this free service came in very usefully in fitting out the expedition of discovery. Columbus was quite satisfied, since he had such good friends at Palos; and he immediately set about choosing the ships.

This, however, did not prove to be quite such a straightforward business as might have been expected. The truth is that, whatever a few monks and physicians may have thought of it, the proposed expedition terrified the ordinary seafaring population of Palos. It was thought to be the wildest and maddest scheme that any one had ever heard of. All that was known about the Atlantic west of the Azores was that it was a sea of darkness, inhabited by monsters and furrowed by enormous waves, and that it fell down the slope of the world so steeply that no ship having once gone down could ever climb up it again. And not only was there reluctance on the part of mariners to engage themselves for the expedition, but also a great shyness on the part of ship-owners to provide ships. This reluctance proved so formidable an impediment that Columbus had to communicate with the King and Queen; with the result that on the

23rd of May the population was summoned to the church of Saint George, where the Notary Public read aloud to them the letter from the sovereigns commanding the port to furnish ships and men, and an additional order summoning the town to obey it immediately. An inducement was provided in the offer of a free pardon to all criminals and persons under sentence who chose to enlist.

Still the thing hung fire; and on June 20 a new and peremptory order was issued by the Crown authorising Columbus to impress the vessels and crew if necessary. Time was slipping away; and in his difficulty Columbus turned to Martin Alonso Pinzon, upon whose influence and power in the town he could count. There were three brothers then in this family—Martin Alonso, Vincenti Yanez, and Francisco Martin, all pilots themselves and owners of ships. These three brothers saw some hope of profit out of the enterprise, and they exerted themselves on Christopher's behalf so thoroughly that, not only did they afford him help in the obtaining of ships, men, and supplies, but they all three decided to go with him.

There was one more financial question to be settled—a question that remains for us in considerable obscurity, but was in all probability partly settled by the aid of these brothers. The total cost of the expedition, consisting of three ships, wages of the crew, stores and provisions, was 1,167,542 maravedis, about L950(in 1900). After all these years of pleading at Court, all the disappointments and deferred hopes and sacrifices made by Columbus, the smallness of this sum cannot but strike us with amazement. Many a nobleman that Columbus must have rubbed shoulders with in his years at Court could have furnished the whole sum out of his pocket and never missed it; yet Columbus had to wait years and years before he could get it from the Crown. Still more amazing, this sum was not all provided by the Crown; 167,000 maravedis were found by Columbus, and the Crown only contributed one million maravedis. One can only assume that Columbus's pertinacity in petitioning the King and Queen to undertake the expedition, when he could with comparative ease have got the money from some of his noble acquaintance, was due to three things—his faith and belief in his Idea, his personal ambition, and his personal greed. He believed in his Idea so thoroughly that he knew he was going to find something across the Atlantic. Continents and islands cannot for long remain in the possession of private persons; they are the currency of crowns; and he did not want to be left in the lurch if the land he hoped to discover should be seized or captured by Spain or Portugal. The result of his discoveries, he was convinced, was going to be far too large a thing to be retained and controlled by any machinery less powerful than that of a kingdom; therefore he was unwilling to accept either preliminary assistance or subsequent rewards from any but the same powerful hand. Admiralties, moreover, and Governor-Generalships and

Viceroyships cannot be conferred by counts and dukes, however powerful; the very title Don could only be conferred by one power in Spain; and all the other titles and dignities that Columbus craved with all his Genoese soul were to be had from the hands of kings, and not from plutocrats. It was characteristic of him all his life never to deal with subordinates, but always to go direct to the head man; and when the whole purpose and ambition of his life was to be put to the test it was only consistent in him, since he could not be independent, to go forth under the protection of the united Crown of Aragon and Castile. Where or how he raised his share of the cost is not known; it is possible that his old friend the Duke of Medina Celi came to his help, or that the Pinzon family, who believed enough in the expedition to risk their lives in it, lent some of the necessary money.

Ever since ships were in danger of going to sea short-handed methods of recruiting and manning them have been very much the same; and there must have been some hot work about the harbour of Palos in the summer of 1492. The place was in a panic. It is highly probable that many of the volunteers were a ruffianly riff-raff from the prisons, to whom personal freedom meant nothing but a chance of plunder; and the recruiting office in Palos must have seen many a picturesque scoundrel coming and taking the oath and making his mark. The presence of these adventurers, many of them entirely ignorant of the sea, would not be exactly an encouragement to the ordinary seaman. It is here very likely that the influence of the Pinzon family was usefully applied. I call it influence, since that is a polite term which covers the application of force in varying degrees; and it was an awkward thing for a Palos sailor to offend the Pinzons, who owned and controlled so much of the shipping in the port. Little by little the preparations went on. In the purchasing of provisions and stores the Pinzons were most helpful to Columbus and, it is not improbable, to themselves also. They also procured the ships; altogether, in the whole history of the fitting out of expeditions, I know nothing since the voyage of the Ark which was so well kept within one family. Moreover it is interesting to notice, since we know the names and places of residence of all the members of the expedition, that the Pinzons, who personally commanded two of the caravels, had them almost exclusively manned by sailors from Palos, while the Admiral's ship was manned by a miscellaneous crew from other places. To be sure they gave the Admiral the biggest ship, but (in his own words) it proved "a dull sailer and unfit for discovery"; while they commanded the two caravels, small and open, but much faster and handier. Clearly these Pinzons will take no harm from a little watching. They may be honest souls enough, but their conduct is just a little suspicious, and we cannot be too careful.

Three vessels were at last secured. The first, named the Santa Maria, was the largest, and was chosen to be the flagship of Columbus. She was of about one hundred tons burden, and would be about ninety feet in length by twenty feet beam. She was decked over, and had a high poop astern and a high forecastle in the bows. She had three masts, two of them square-rigged, with a latine sail on the mizzen mast; and she carried a crew of fifty-two persons. Where and how they all stowed themselves away is a matter upon which we can only make wondering guesses; for this ship was about the size of an ordinary small coasting schooner, such as is worked about the coasts of these islands with a crew of six or eight men. The next largest ship was the Pinta, which was commanded by Martin Alonso Pinzon, who took his brother Francisco with him as sailing-master. The Pinta was of fifty tons burden, decked only at the bow and stern, and the fastest of the three ships; she also had three masts. The third ship was a caravel of forty tons and called the Nina; she belonged to Juan Nino of Palos. She was commanded by Vincenti Pinzon, and had a complement of eighteen men. Among the crew of the flagship, whose names and places of residence are to be found in the Appendix, were an Englishman and an Irishman. The Englishman is entered as Tallarte de Lajes (Ingles), who has been ingeniously identified with a possible Allard or AEthelwald of Winchelsea, there having been several generations of Allards who were sailors of Winchelsea in the fifteenth century. Sir Clements Markham thinks that this Allard may have been trading to Coruna and have married and settled down at Lajes. There is also Guillermo Ires, an Irishman from Galway.

Allard and William, shuffling into the recruiting office in Palos, doubtless think that this is a strange place for them to meet, and rather a wild business that they are embarked upon, among all these bloody Spaniards. Some how I feel more confidence in Allard than in William, knowing, as I do so well, this William of Galway, whether on his native heath or in the strange and distant parts of the world to which his sanguine temperament leads him. Alas, William, you are but the first of a mighty stream that will leave the Old Country for the New World; the world destined to be good for the fortunes of many from the Old Country, but for the Old Country itself not good. Little does he know, drunken William, willing to be on hand where there is adventure brewing, and to be after going with the boys and getting his health on the salt water, what a path of hope for those who go, and of heaviness for those who stay behind, he is opening up . . . . Farewell, William; I hope you were not one of those whom they let out of gaol.

June slid into July, and still the preparations were not complete. Down on the mud banks of the Tinto, where at low water the vessels were left high and dry, and where the caulking and refitting were in hand, there was trouble with the workmen. Gomaz

Rascon and Christoval Quintero, the owners of the Pinta, who had resented her being pressed into the service, were at the bottom of a good deal of it. Things could not be found; gear mysteriously gave way after it had been set up; the caulking was found to have been carelessly and imperfectly done; and when the caulkers were commanded to do it over again they decamped. Even the few volunteers, the picked hands upon whom Columbus was relying, gave trouble. In those days of waiting there was too much opportunity for talk in the shore-side wine-shops; some of the volunteers repented and tried to cry off their bargains; others were dissuaded by their relatives, and deserted and hid themselves. No mild measures were of any use; a reign of terror had to be established; and nothing short of the influence of the Pinzons was severe enough to hold the company together. To these vigorous measures, however, all opposition gradually yielded. By the end of July the provisions and stores were on board, the whole complement of eighty-seven persons collected and enlisted, and only the finishing touches left for Columbus. It is a sign of the distrust and fear evinced with regard to this expedition, that no priest accompanied it—something of a sorrow to pious Christopher, who would have liked his chaplain. There were two surgeons, or barbers, and a physician; there were an overseer, a secretary, a master-at-arms; there was an interpreter to speak to the natives of the new lands in Hebrew, Greek, German, Chaldean or Arabic; and there was an assayer and silversmith to test the quality of the precious metals that they were sure to find. Up at La Rabida, with the busy and affectionate assistance of the old Prior, Columbus made his final preparations. Ferdinand was to stay at Cordova with Beatriz, and to go to school there; while Diego was already embarked upon his life's voyage, having been appointed a page to the Queen's son, Prince Juan, and handed over to the care of some of the Court ladies. The course to be sailed was talked over and over again; the bearings and notes of the pilot at Porto Santo consulted and discussed; and a chart was made by Columbus himself, and copied with his own hands for use on the three ships.

On the 2nd of August everything was ready; the ships moored out in the stream, the last stragglers of the crew on board, the last sack of flour and barrel of beef stowed away. Columbus confessed himself to the Prior of La Rabida—a solemn moment for him in the little chapel up on the pine-clad hill. His last evening ashore would certainly be spent at the monastery, and his last counsels taken with Perez and Doctor Hernandez. We can hardly realise the feelings of Christopher on the eve of his departure from the land where all his roots were, to a land of mere faith and conjecture. Even today, when the ocean is furrowed by crowded highways, and the earth is girdled with speaking wires, and distances are so divided and reduced that the traveller need never be very long out of touch with his home, few people can set out on a long voyage without some emotional disturbance, however slight it may be; and to Columbus on this night the little town upon which he looked down from the monastery, which had been the scene of so many delays and difficulties and vexations, must have seemed suddenly dear and familiar to him as he realised that after to-morrow its busy and well-known scenes might be for ever a thing of the past to him. Behind him, living or dead, lay all he humanly loved and cared for; before him lay a voyage full of certain difficulties and dangers; dangers from the ships, dangers from the crews, dangers from the weather, dangers from the unknown path itself; and beyond them, a twinkling star on the horizon of his hopes, lay the land of his belief. That he meant to arrive there and to get back again was beyond all doubt his firm intention; and in the simple grandeur of that determination the weaknesses of character that were grouped about it seem unimportant. In this starlit hour among the pine woods his life came to its meridian; everything that was him was at its best and greatest there. Beneath him, on the talking tide of the river, lay the ships and equipment that represented years of steady effort and persistence; before him lay the pathless ocean which he meant to cross by the inner light of his faith. What he had suffered, he had suffered by himself; what he had won, he had won by himself; what he was to finish, he would finish by himself.

But the time for meditations grows short. Lights are moving about in the town beneath; there is an unwonted midnight stir and bustle; the whole population is up and about, running hither and thither with lamps and torches through the starlit night. The tide is flowing; it will be high water before dawn; and with the first of the ebb the little fleet is to set sail. The stream of hurrying sailors and townspeople sets towards the church of Saint George, where mass is to be said and the Sacrament administered to the voyagers. The calls and shouts die away; the bell stops ringing; and the low muttering voice of the priest is heard beginning the Office. The light of the candles shines upon the gaudy roof, and over the altar upon the wooden image of Saint George vanquishing the dragon, upon which the eyes of Christopher rested during some part of the service, and where to-day your eyes may rest also if you make that pilgrimage. The moment approaches; the bread and the wine are consecrated; there is a shuffling of knees and feet; and then a pause. The clear notes of the bell ring out upon the warm dusky silence—once, twice, thrice; the living God and the cold presence of dawn enter the church together. Every head is bowed; and for once at least every heart of that company beats in unison with the rest. And then the Office goes on, and the dark-skinned congregation streams up to the sanctuary and receives the Communion, while the blue light of dawn increases and the candles pale before the coming day. And then out again to the boats with shoutings and farewells, for the tide has now turned; hoisting of sails and tripping of anchors and breaking out of gorgeous ensigns; and the ships are moving! The Maria leads, with the sign of the Redemption painted on her mainsail and the standard of Castile flying at her mizzen; and there is cheering from ships and from shore, and a faint sound of bells from the town of Huelva.

Thus, the sea being—calm, and a fresh breeze blowing off the land, did Christopher Columbus set sail from Palos at sunrise on Friday the 3rd of August 1492.

CHAPTER XIII

EVENTS OF THE FIRST VOYAGE

"In nomine D.N. Jesu Christi—Friday, August 3, 1492, at eight o'clock we started from the bar of Saltes. We went with a strong sea breeze sixty miles,—[Columbus reckoned in Italian miles, of which four = one league.]—which are fifteen leagues, towards the south, until sunset: afterwards to the south-west and to the south, quarter south-west, which was the way to the Canaries."

With these rousing words the Journal

[The account of Columbus's first voyage is taken from a Journal written by himself, but which in its original form does not exist. Las Casas had it in his possession, but as he regarded it (no doubt with justice) as too voluminous and discursive to be interesting, he made an abridged edition, in which the exact words of Columbus were sometimes quoted, but which for the most part is condensed into a narrative in the third person. This abridged Journal, consisting of seventy-six closely written folios, was first published by Navarrette in 1825. When Las Casas wrote his 'Historie,' however, he appears here and there to have restored sections of the original Journal into the abridged one; and many of these restorations are of importance. If the whole account of his voyage written by Columbus himself were available in its exact form I would print it here; but as it is not, I think it better to continue my narrative, simply using the Journal of Las Casas as a document.]

of Columbus's voyage begins; and they sound a salt and mighty chord which contains the true diapason of the symphony of his voyages. There could not have been a more fortunate beginning, with clear weather and a calm sea, and the wind in exactly the right quarter. On Saturday and Sunday the same conditions held, so there was time and opportunity for the three very miscellaneous ships' companies to shake down into something like order, and for all the elaborate discipline of sea life to be arranged and established; and we may employ the interval by noting what aids to navigation Columbus had at his disposal.

The chief instrument was the astrolabe, which was an improvement on the primitive quadrant then in use for taking the altitude of the sun. The astrolabe, it will be remembered, had been greatly improved, by Martin Behaim and the Portuguese Commission in 1840—[1440 D.W.]; and it was this instrument, a simplification of the astrolabe used in astronomy ashore, that Columbus chiefly used in getting his

---

34

solar altitudes. As will be seen from the illustration, its broad principle was that of a metal circle with a graduated circumference and two arms pivoted in the centre. It was made as heavy as possible; and in using it the observer sat on deck with his back against the mainmast and with his left hand held up the instrument by the ring at the top. The long arm was moved round until the two sights fixed upon it were on with the sun. The point where the other arm then cut the circle gave the altitude. In conjunction with this instrument were used the tables of solar declination compiled by Regiomontanus, and covering the sun's declination between the years 1475 and 1566.

The compass in Columbus's day existed, so far as all essentials are concerned, as it exists to-day. Although it lacked the refinements introduced by Lord Kelvin it was swung in double-cradles, and had the thirty-two points painted upon a card. The discovery of the compass, and even of the lodestone, are things wrapt in obscurity; but the lodestone had been known since at least the eleventh century, and the compass certainly since the thirteenth. With the compass were used the sea charts, which were simply maps on a rather larger and more exact scale than the land maps of the period. There were no soundings or currents marked on the old charts, which were drawn on a plane projection; and they can have been of little—practical use to navigators except in the case of coasts which were elaborately charted on a large scale. The chart of Columbus, in so far as it was concerned with the ocean westward of the Azores, can of course have contained nothing except the conjectured islands or lands which he hoped to find; possibly the land seen by the shipwrecked pilot may have been marked on it, and his failure to find that land may have been the reason why, as we shall see, he changed his course to the southward on the 7th of October. It must be remembered that Columbus's conception of the world was that of the Portuguese Mappemonde of 1490, a sketch of which is here reproduced. This conception of the world excluded the Pacific Ocean and the continent of North and South America, and made it reasonable to suppose that any one who sailed westward long enough from Spain would ultimately reach Cathay and the Indies. Behaim's globe, which was completed in the year 1492, represented the farthest point that geographical knowledge had reached previous to the discoveries of Columbus, and on it is shown the island of Cipango or Japan.

By far the most important element in the navigation of Columbus, in so far as estimating his position was concerned, was what is known as "dead-reckoning" that is to say, the computation of the distance travelled by the ship through the water. At present this distance is measured by a patent log, which in its commonest form is a propeller-shaped instrument trailed through the water at the end of a long wire or cord the inboard end of which is attached to a registering clock. On being dragged through the water the propeller spins round and the twisting action is communicated by the cord to the clock-work machinery which counts the miles. In the case of powerful steamers and in ordinary weather dead-reckoning is very accurately calculated by the number of revolutions of the propellers recorded in the engine-room; and a device not unlike this was known to the Romans in the time of the Republic. They attached small wheels about four feet in diameter to the sides of their ships; the passage of the water turned the wheels, and a very simple gearing was arranged which threw a pebble into a tallypot at each revolution. This device, however, seems to have been abandoned or forgotten in Columbus's day, when there was no more exact method of estimating dead-reckoning than the primitive one of spitting over the side in calm weather, or at other times throwing some object into the water and estimating the rate of progress by its speed in passing the ship's side. The hour-glass, which was used to get the multiple for long distances, was of course the only portable time measurer available for Columbus. These, with a rough knowledge of astronomy, and the taking of the altitude of the polar star, were the only known means for ascertaining the position of his ship at sea.

The first mishap occurred on Monday, August 6th, when the Pinta carried away her rudder. The Pinta, it will be remembered, was commanded by Martin Alonso Pinzon, and was owned by Gomaz Rascon and Christoval Quintero, who had been at the bottom of some of the troubles ashore; and it was thought highly probable that these two rascals had something to do with the mishap, which they had engineered in the hope that their vessel would be left behind at the Canaries. Martin Alonso, however, proved a man of resource, and rigged up a sort of steering gear with ropes. There was a choppy sea, and Columbus could not bring his own vessel near enough to render any assistance, though he doubtless bawled his directions to Pinzon, and looked with a troubled eye on the commotion going on on board the Pinta. On the next day the jury-rigged rudder carried away again, and was again repaired, but it was decided to try and make the island of Lanzarote in the Canaries, and to get another caravel to replace the Pinta. All through the next day the Santa Maria and the Nina had to shorten sail in order not to leave the damaged Pinta behind; the three captains had a discussion and difference of opinion as to where they were; but Columbus, who was a genius at dead-reckoning, proved to be right in his surmise, and they came in sight of the Canaries on Thursday morning, August 9th.

Columbus left Pinzon on the Grand Canary with orders to try to obtain a caravel there, while he sailed on to Gomera, which he reached on Sunday night, with a similar purpose. As he was unsuccessful he sent a message by a boat that was going back to tell Pinzon to beach the Pinta and repair her rudder; and having spent more days in fruitless search for a vessel, he started back to join Pinzon on August 23rd. During the night he passed the Peak of Teneriffe, which was then in eruption. The repairs to the Pinta, doubtless in no way expedited by Messrs. Rascon and Quintera, took longer than had been expected; it was found necessary to make an entirely new rudder for her; and advantage was taken of the delay to make some alterations in the rig of the Nina, which was changed from a latine rig to a square rig, so that she might be better able to keep up with the others. September had come before these two jobs were completed; and on the 2nd of September the three ships sailed for Gomera, the most westerly of the islands, where they anchored in the north-east bay. The Admiral was in a great hurry to get away from the islands and from the track of merchant ships, for he had none too much confidence in the integrity of his crews, which were already murmuring and finding every mishap a warning sign from God. He therefore only stayed long enough at Gomera to take in wood and water and provisions, and set sail from that island on the 6th of September.

The wind fell lighter and lighter, and on Friday the little fleet lay becalmed within sight of Ferro. But on Saturday evening north-east airs sprang up again, and they were able to make nine leagues of westing. On Sunday they had lost sight of land; and at thus finding their ships three lonely specks in the waste of ocean the crew lost heart and began to lament. There was something like a panic, many of the sailors bursting into tears and imploring Columbus to take them home again. To us it may seem a rather childish exhibition; but it must be remembered that these sailors were unwillingly embarked upon a voyage which they believed would only lead to death and disaster. The bravest of us to-day, if he found himself press-ganged on board a balloon and embarked upon a journey, the object of which was to land upon Mars or the moon, might find it difficult to preserve his composure on losing sight of the earth; and the parallel is not too extreme to indicate the light in which their present enterprise must have appeared to many of the Admiral's crew.

Columbus gave orders to the captains of the other two ships that, in case of separation, they were to sail westward for 700 leagues-that being the distance at which he evidently expected to find land—and there to lie-to from midnight until morning. On this day also, seeing the temper of the sailors, he began one of the crafty stratagems upon which he prided himself, and which were often undoubtedly of great use to him; he kept two reckonings, one a true one, which he entered in his log, and one a false one, by means of which the distance run was made out to be less than what it actually was, so that in case he could not make land as soon as he hoped the crew would not be unduly discouraged. In other words, he wished to have a margin at the other end, for he did not want a mutiny when he was perhaps within a few leagues of his destination. On this day he notes that the raw and inexperienced seamen were giving trouble in other ways, and steering very badly, continually letting the ship's head fall off to the north; and many must have been the angry remonstrances from the captain to the man at the wheel. Altogether rather a trying day for Christopher, who surely has about as much on his hands as ever mortal had; but he knows how to handle ships and how to handle sailors, and so long as this ten-knot breeze lasts, he can walk the high poop of the Santa Maria with serenity, and snap his fingers at the dirty rabble below.

On Monday they made sixty leagues, the Admiral duly announcing forty-eight; on Tuesday twenty leagues, published as sixteen; and on this day they saw a large piece of a mast which had evidently belonged to a ship of at least 120 tons burden. This was not an altogether cheerful sight for the eighteen souls on board the little Nina, who wondered ruefully what was going to happen to them of forty tons when ships three times their size had evidently been unable to live in this abominable sea!

On Thursday, September 13th, when Columbus took his observations, he made a great scientific discovery, although he did not know it at the time. He noticed that the needle of the compass was declining to the west of north instead of having a slight declination to the east of north, as all mariners knew it to have. In other words, he had passed the line of true north and of no variation, and must therefore have been in latitude 28 deg. N. and longitude 29 deg. 37' W. of Greenwich. With his usual secrecy he said nothing about it; perhaps he was waiting to see if the pilots on the other ships had noticed it, but apparently they were not so exact in their observations as he was. On the next day, Friday, the wind falling a little lighter, they, made only twenty leagues. "Here the persons on the caravel Nina said they had seen a jay and a ringtail, and these birds never come more than twenty-five leagues from land at most." —Unhappy "persons on the Nina"! Nineteen souls, including the captain, afloat in a very small boat, and arguing God knows what from the fact that a jay and a ringtail never went more than twenty-five leagues from land!—The next day also was not without its incident; for on Saturday evening they saw a meteor, or "marvellous branch of fire" falling from the serene violet of the sky into the sea.

They were now well within the influence of the trade-wind, which in these months blows steadily from the east, and maintains an exquisite and balmy climate. Even the Admiral, never very communicative about his sensations, deigns to mention them here, and is reported to have said that "it was a great pleasure to enjoy the morning; that nothing was lacking except to hear the nightingales, and that the weather was like

April in Andalusia." On this day they saw some green grasses, which the Admiral considered must have floated off from some island; "not the continent," says the Admiral, whose theories are not to be disturbed by a piece of grass, "because I make the continental land farther onward." The crew, ready to take the most depressing and pessimistic view of everything, considered that the lumps of grass belonged to rocks or submerged lands, and murmured disparaging things about the Admiral. As a matter of fact these grasses were masses of seaweed detached from the Sargasso Sea, which they were soon to enter.

On Monday, September 17th, four days after Columbus had noted it, the other pilots noted the declination of the needle, which they had found on taking the position of the North star. They did not like it; and Columbus, whose knowledge of astronomy came to his aid, ordered them to take the position of the North star at dawn again, which they did, and found that the needles were true. He evidently thought it useless to communicate to them his scientific speculations, so he explained to them that it was the North star which was moving in its circle, and not the compass. One is compelled to admit that in these little matters of deceit the Admiral always shone. To-day, among the seaweed on the ship's side, he picked up a little crayfish, which he kept for several days, presumably in a bottle in his cabin; and perhaps afterwards ate.

So for several days this calm and serene progress westward was maintained. The trade-wind blew steady and true, balmy and warm also; the sky was cloudless, except at morning and evening dusk; and there were for scenery those dazzling expanses of sea and sky, and those gorgeous hues of dawn and sunset, which are only to be found in the happy latitudes. The things that happened to them, the bits of seaweed and fishes that they saw in the water, the birds that flew around them, were observed with a wondering attention and wistful yearning after their meaning such as is known only to children and to sailors adventuring on uncharted seas. The breezes were milder even than those of the Canaries, and the waters always less salt; and the men, forgetting their fears of the monsters of the Sea of Darkness, would bathe alongside in the limpid blue. The little crayfish was a "sure indication of land"; a tunny fish, killed by the company on the Nina, was taken to be an indication from the west, "where I hope in that exalted God, in whose hands are all victories, that land will very soon appear"; they saw another ringtail, "which is not accustomed to sleep on the sea"; two pelicans came to the ship, "which was an indication that land was near"; a large dark cloud appeared to the north, "which is a sign that land is near"; they saw one day a great deal of grass, "although the previous day they had not seen any"; they took a bird with their hands which was like a jay; "it was a river bird and not a sea bird"; they saw a whale, "which is an indication that they are near land, because they always remain near it"; afterwards a pelican came from the west-north-west and went to the south-east, "which was an indication that it left land to the west-north-west, because these birds sleep on land and in the morning they come to the sea in search of food, and do not go twenty leagues from land." And "at dawn two or three small land birds came singing to the ships; and afterwards disappeared before sunrise."

Such beautiful signs, interpreted by the light of their wishes, were the events of this part of the voyage. In the meantime, they have their little differences. Martin Alonso Pinzon, on Tuesday, September 18th, speaks from the Pinta to the Santa Maria, and says that he will not wait for the others, but will go and make the land, since it is so near; but apparently he does not get very far out of the way, the wind which wafts him wafting also the Santa Maria and the Nina.

On September the 19th there was a comparison of dead-reckonings. The Nina's pilot made it 440 leagues from the Canaries, the Pinta's 420 leagues, and the Admiral's pilot, doubtless instructed by the Admiral, made it 400. On Sunday the 23rd they were getting into the seaweed and finding crayfish again; and there being no reasonable cause for complaint a scare was got up among the crew on an exceedingly ingenious point. The wind having blown steadily from the east for a matter of three weeks, they said that it would never blow in any other direction, and that they would never be able to get back to Spain; but later in the afternoon the sea got up from the westward, as though in answer to their fears, and as if to prove that somewhere or other ahead of them there was a west wind blowing; and the Admiral remarks that "the high sea was very necessary to me, as it came to pass once before in the time when the Jews went out of Egypt with Moses, who took them from captivity." And indeed there was something of Moses in this man, who thus led his little rabble from a Spanish seaport out across the salt wilderness of the ocean, and interpreted the signs for them, and stood between them and the powers of vengeance and terror that were set about their uncharted path.

But it appears that the good Admiral had gone just a little too far in interpreting everything they saw as a sign that they were approaching land; for his miserable crew, instead of being comforted by this fact, now took the opportunity to be angry because the signs were not fulfilled. The more the signs pointed to their nearness to land, the more they began to murmur and complain because they did not see it. They began to form together in little groups—always an ominous sign at sea —and even at night those who were not on deck got together in murmuring companies. Some, of the things that they said, indeed, were not very far from the truth; among others, that it was "a great madness on their part to venture their lives in following out the madness of a foreigner who to make himself a great lord had risked his life, and now saw himself and all of them in great exigency and was deceiving so many people." They remembered that his proposition, or "dream" as they not inaptly call it, had been contradicted by many great and lettered men; and then followed some very ominous words indeed. They held

[The substance of these murmurings is not in the abridged Journal, but is given by Las Casas under the date of September 24.]

that "it was enough to excuse them from whatever might be done in the matter that they had arrived where man had never dared to navigate, and that they were not obliged to go to the end of the world, especially as, if they delayed more, they would not be able to have provisions to return." In short, the best thing would be to throw him into the sea some night, and make a story that he had fallen, into the water while taking the position of a star with his astrolabe; and no one would ask any questions, as he was a foreigner. They carried this talk to the Pinzons, who listened to them; after all, we have not had to wait long for trouble with the Pinzons! "Of these Pinzons Christopher Columbus complains greatly, and of the trouble they had given him."

There is only one method of keeping down mutiny at sea, and of preserving discipline. It is hard enough where the mutineers are all on one ship and the commander's officers are loyal to him; but when they are distributed over three ships, the captains of two of which are willing to listen to them, the problem becomes grave indeed. We have no details of how Columbus quieted them; but it is probable that his strong personality awed them, while his clever and plausible words persuaded them. He was the best sailor of them all and they knew it; and in a matter of this kind the best and strongest man always wins, and can only in a pass of this kind maintain his authority by proving his absolute right to it. So he talked and persuaded and bullied and encouraged and cheered them; "laughing with them," as Las Casas says, "while he was weeping at heart."

Probably as a result of this unpleasantness there was on the following day, Tuesday, September 25th, a consultation between: Martin Alonso Pinzon and the Admiral. The Santa Maria closed up with the Pinta, and a chart was passed over on a cord. There were islands marked on the chart in this region, possibly the islands reported by the shipwrecked pilot, possibly the island of Antilla; and Pinzon said he thought that they were somewhere in the region of them, and the Admiral said that he thought so too. There was a deal of talk and pricking of positions on charts; and then, just as the sun was setting, Martin Alonso, standing on the stern of the Pinta, raised a shout and said that he saw land; asking (business-like Martin) at the same time for the reward which had been promised to the first one who should see land: They all saw it, a low cloud to the southwest, apparently about twenty-five leagues distant; and honest Christopher, in the emotion of the moment, fell on his knees in gratitude to God. The crimson sunset of that evening saw the rigging of the three ships black with eager figures, and on the quiet air were borne the sounds of the Gloria in Excelsis, which was repeated by each ship's company.

The course was altered to the south-west, and they sailed in that direction seventeen leagues during the night; but in the morning there was no land to be seen. The sunset clouds that had so often deceived the dwellers in the Canaries and the Azores, and that in some form or other hover at times upon all eagerly scanned horizons, had also deceived Columbus and every one of his people; but they created a diversion which was of help to the Admiral in getting things quiet again, for which in his devout soul he thanked the merciful providence of God.

And so they sailed on again on a westward course. They were still in the Sargasso Sea, and could watch the beautiful golden floating mass of the gulf-weed, covered with berries and showing, a little way under the clear water, bright green leaves. The sea was as smooth as the river in Seville; there were frigate pelicans flying about, and John Dorys in the water; several gulls were seen; and a youth on board the Nina killed a pelican with a stone. On Monday, October 1st, there was a heavy shower of rain; and Juan de la Cosa, Columbus's pilot, came up to him with the doleful information that they had run 578 leagues from the island of Ferro. According to Christopher's doctored reckoning the distance published was 584 leagues; but his true reckoning, about which he said nothing to a soul, showed that they had gone 707 leagues. The breeze still kept steady and the sea calm; and day after day, with the temper of the crews getting uglier and uglier, the three little vessels forged westward through the blue, weed-strewn waters, their tracks lying undisturbed far behind them. On Saturday, October 6th, the Admiral was signalled by Alonso Pinzon, who wanted to change the course to the south-west. It appears that, having failed to find the, islands of the shipwrecked pilot, they were now making for the island of Cipango, and that this request of Pinzon had something to do with some theory of his that they had better turn to the south to reach that island; while Columbus's idea now evidently was—to push straight on to the mainland of Cathay. Columbus had his way; but the grumbling and murmuring in creased among the crew.

On the next day, Sunday, and perhaps just in time to avert another outbreak, there was heard the sound of a gun, and the watchers on the Santa Maria and the Pinta saw a puff of smoke coming from the Nina, which was sailing ahead, and hoisting a flag on her masthead. This was the signal agreed upon for the discovery of land, and it seemed as though their search was at last at an end. But it was a mistake. In the afternoon the land that the people of the Nina thought they had seen had disappeared, and the horizon was empty except for a great flight of birds that was seen passing from the north to the south-west. The Admiral, remembering how often birds had guided the Portuguese in the islands in their possessions, argued that the birds were either going to sleep on land or were perhaps flying from winter, which he assumed to be approaching in the land from whence they came. He therefore altered. his course from west to west-south-west. This course was entered upon an hour before sunset and continued throughout the night and the next day. "The sea was like the river of Seville," says the Admiral; "the breezes as soft as at Seville in April, and very fragrant." More birds were to be seen, and there were many signs of land; but the crew, so often disappointed in their hopeful interpretations of the phenomena surrounding them, kept on murmuring and complaining. On Tuesday, October 9th, the wind chopped round a little and the course was altered, first to south-west and then at evening to a point north of west; and the journal records that "all night they heard birds passing." The next day Columbus resumed the west-southwesterly course and made a run of fifty-nine leagues; but the mariners broke out afresh in their discontent, and declined to go any farther. They complained of the long voyage, and expressed their views strongly to the commander. But they had to deal with a man who was determined to begin with, and who saw in the many signs of land that they had met with only an additional inducement to go on. He told them firmly that with or without their consent he intended to go on until he had found the land he had come to seek.

The next day, Thursday, October 11th, was destined to be for ever memorable in the history of the world. It began ordinarily enough, with a west-south-west wind blowing fresh, and on a sea rather rougher than they had had lately. The people on the Santa Maria saw some petrels and a green branch in the water; the Pinta saw a reed and two small sticks carved with iron, and one or two other pieces of reeds and grasses that had been grown on shore, as well as a small board. Most wonderful of all, the people of the Nina saw "a little branch full of dog roses"; and it would be hard to estimate the sweet significance of this fragment of a wild plant from land to the senses of men who had been so long upon a sea from which they had thought never to land alive. The day drew to its close; and after nightfall, according to their custom, the crew of the ships repeated the Salve Regina. Afterwards the Admiral addressed the people and sailors of his ship, "very merry and pleasant," reminding them of the favours God had shown them with regard to the weather, and begging them, as they hoped to see land very soon, within an hour or so, to keep an extra good look-out that night from the forward forecastle; and adding to the reward of an annuity of 10,000 maravedis, offered by the Queen to whoever should sight land first, a gift on his own account of a silk doublet.

The moon was in its third quarter, and did not rise until eleven o'clock. The first part of the night was dark, and there was only a faint starlight into which the anxious eyes of the look-out men peered from the forecastles of the three ships. At ten o'clock Columbus was walking on the poop of his vessel, when he suddenly saw a light right ahead. The light seemed to rise and fall as though it were a candle or a lantern held in some one's hand and waved up and down. The Admiral called Pedro Gutierrez to him and asked him whether he saw anything; and he also saw the light. Then he sent for Rodrigo Sanchez and asked him if he saw the light; but he did not, perhaps because from where he was standing it was occulted. But the others were left in no doubt, for the light was seen once or twice more, and to the eyes of the anxious little group standing on the high stern deck of the Santa Maria it appeared unmistakably. The Nina was not close at hand, and the Pinta had gone on in front hoping to make good her mistake; but there was no doubt on board the Santa Maria that the light which they had seen was a light like a candle or a torch waved slowly up and down. They lost the light again; and as the hours in that night stole away and the moon rose slowly in the sky the seamen on the Santa Maria must have almost held their breath.

At about two o'clock in the morning the sound of a gun was heard from the Pinta, who could be seen hoisting her flags; Rodrigo de Triana, the look-out on board of her, having reported land in sight; and there sure enough in the dim light lay the low shores of an island a few miles ahead of them.

Immediately all sails were lowered, except a small trysail which enabled the ships to lie-to and stand slowly off and on, waiting for the daylight. I suppose there was never a longer night than that; but dawn came at last, flooding the sky with lemon and saffron and scarlet and orange, until at last the pure gold of the sun glittered on the water. And when it rose it showed the sea-weary mariners an island lying in the blue sea ahead of them: the island of Guanahani; San Salvador, as it was christened by Columbus; or, to give it its modern name, Watling's Island.

CHAPTER XIV

LANDFALL

During the night the ships had drifted a little with the current, and before the north-east wind. When the look-out man on the Pinta first reported land in sight it was probably the north-east corner of the island, where the land rises to a height of 120 feet, that he saw. The actual anchorage of Columbus was most likely to the westward of the island; for there was a strong north-easterly breeze, and as the whole of the eastern coast is fringed by a barrier reef, he would not risk his ships on a lee shore. Finding himself off the north end of the island at sunrise, the most natural thing for him to do, on making sail again, would be to stand southward along the west side of the island looking for an anchorage. The first few miles of the shore have rocky exposed points, and the bank where there is shoal water only extends half a mile from the shore. Immediately beyond that the bottom shelves rapidly down to a depth of 2000 fathoms, so that if Columbus was sounding as he came south he would find no bottom there. Below what are called the Ridings Rocks, however, the land sweeps to the south and east in a long sheltered bay, and to the south of these rocks there is good anchorage and firm holding-ground in about eight fathoms of water.

We may picture them, therefore, approaching this land in the bright sunshine of the early morning, their ears, that had so long heard nothing but the slat of canvas and the rush and bubble of water under the prows, filled at last with the great resounding roar of the breakers on the coral reef; their eyes, that had so long looked upon blue emptiness and the star-spangled violet arch of night, feasting upon the living green of the foliage ashore; and the easterly breeze carrying to their eager nostrils the perfumes of land. Amid an excitement and joyful anticipation that it is exhilarating even to think about the cables were got up and served and coiled on deck, and the anchors, which some of them had thought would never grip the bottom again, unstopped and cleared. The leadsman of the Santa Maria, who has been finding no bottom with his forty-fathom line, suddenly gets a sounding; the water shoals rapidly until the nine-fathom mark is unwetted, and the lead comes up with its bottom covered with brown ooze. Sail is shortened; one after another the great ungainly sheets of canvas are clewed up or lowered down on deck; one after another the three helms are starboarded, and the three ships brought up to the wind. Then with three mighty splashes that send the sea birds whirling and screaming above the rocks the anchors go down; and the Admiral stands on his high poop-deck, and looks long and searchingly at the fragment of earth, rock-rimmed, surf-fringed, and tree-crowned, of which he is Viceroy and Governor-General.

Watling's Island, as it is now called, or San Salvador, as Columbus named it, or Guanahani, as it was known to the aborigines, is situated in latitude 24 deg. 6' N., and longitude 74 deg 26' W., and is an irregularly shaped white sandstone islet in about the middle of the great Bahama Bank. The space occupied by the whole group is shaped like an irregular triangle extending from the Navidad Bank in the Caribbean Sea at the south-east corner, to Bahama Island in Florida Strait on the north, about 200 miles. The south side trends west by north for 600 miles, and the north side north-west by north 720 miles. Most of the islands and small rocks in this group, called Keys or Cays, are very low, and rise only a few feet above the sea; the highest is about 400 feet high. They are generally situated on the edge of coral and sand banks, some of which are of a very dangerous character. They are thinly wooded, except in the case of one or two of the larger islands which contain timber of moderate dimensions. The climate of the Bahamas is mild and temperate, with refreshing sea breezes in the hottest months; and there is a mean temperature of 75 deg. from November to April. Watling's Island is about twelve miles in length by six in breadth, with rocky shores slightly indented. The greater part of its area is occupied by salt-water lagoons, separated from one another by small wooded hills from too to 140 feet high. There is plenty of grass; indeed the island is now considered to be the most fertile in the Bahamas, and raises an excellent breed of cattle and sheep. In common with the other islands of the group it was originally settled by the Spaniards, and afterwards by the British, who were driven from the Bahamas again by the Spanish in the year 1641. After a great deal of changing hands they were ceded to Great Britain in 1783, and have remained in her possession ever since. In 1897 the population of the whole group was estimated at 52,000 the whites being in the proportion of one to six of the coloured population. Watling's Island contains about 600 inhabitants scattered over the surface, with a small settlement called Cockburn Town on the west side, nearly opposite the landfall of Columbus. The seat of the local government is in the island of New Providence, and the inhabitants of Watling's Island and of Rum Cay unite in sending one representative to the House of Assembly. It is high water, full and change, at Watling's Island at 7 h. 40 m., as it was in the days of Columbus; and these facts form about the sum of the world's knowledge of and interest in Watling's Island to-day.

But it was a different matter on Friday morning, October 12, 1492,

[This date is reckoned in the old style. The true astronomical date would be October 21st, which is the modern anniversary of the discovery]

when, all having been made snug on board the Santa Maria, the Admiral of the Ocean Seas put on his armour and his scarlet cloak over it and prepared to go ashore. The boat was lowered and manned by a crew well armed, and Columbus took with him Rodrigo de Escovedo, the secretary to the expedition, and Rodrigo Sanchez his overseer; they also took on board Martin Alonso Pinzon and Vincenti Yanez Pinzon, the captains of the other two ships. As they rowed towards the shore they saw a few naked inhabitants, who hid themselves at their approach. Columbus carried with him the royal standard, and the two captains each had a banner of the expedition, which was a square flag with an "F" and a "Y" upon either side, each letter being surmounted by the crown of the sovereigns and a green cross covering the whole. Columbus assembled his little band around him and called upon them to bear witness that in the presence of them all he was taking possession of the island for the King and Queen of Spain; duly making depositions in writing on the spot, and having them signed and witnessed. Then he gave the name of San Salvador to the island and said a prayer; and while this solemn little ceremony was in progress, the astonished natives crept out of their hiding and surrounded the strange white men. They gesticulated and grovelled and pointed upwards, as though this gang of armed and bearded Spaniards, with the tall white-bearded Italian in the midst of them, had fallen from the skies.

The first interest of the voyagers was in the inhabitants of this delightful land. They found them well built, athletic-looking men, most of them young, with handsome bodies and intelligent faces. Columbus, eager to begin his missionary work, gave them some red caps and some glass beads, with which he found them so delighted that he had good hopes of making converts, and from which he argued that "they were a people who would better be freed and converted to our Holy Faith by love than by force," which sentence of his contains within itself the whole missionary spirit of the time. These natives, who were the freest people in the world, were to be "freed"; freed or saved from the darkness of their happy innocence and brought to the light of a religion that had just evolved the Inquisition; freed by love if possible, and by red caps and glass beads; if not possible, then freed by force and with guns; but freed they were to be at all costs. It is a tragic thought that, at the very first impact of the Old World upon this Eden of the West, this dismal error was set on foot and the first links in the chain of slavery forged. But for the moment nothing of it was perceptible; nothing but red caps and glass beads, and trinkets and toys, and freeing by love. The sword that Columbus held out to them, in order to find out if they knew the use of weapons, they innocently grasped by the blade and so cut their fingers; and that sword, extended with knowledge and grasped with fearless ignorance, is surely an emblem of the spread of civilisation and of its doubtful blessings in the early stages. Let us hear Columbus himself, as he recorded his first impression of Guanahani:

"Further, it appeared to me that they were a very poor people, in everything. They all go naked as their mothers gave them birth, and the women also, although I only saw one of the latter who was very young, and all those whom I saw were young men, none more than thirty years of age. They were very well built with very handsome bodies, and very good faces. Their hair was almost as coarse as horses' tails, and short, and they wear it over the eyebrows, except a small quantity behind, which they wear long and never cut. Some paint themselves blackish, and they are of the colour of the inhabitants of the Canaries, neither black nor white, and some paint themselves white, some red, some whatever colour they find: and some paint their faces, some all the body, some only the eyes, and some only the nose. They do not carry arms nor know what they are, because I showed them swords and they took them by the edge and ignorantly cut themselves. They have no iron: their spears are sticks without iron, and some of them have a fish's tooth at the end and others have other things. They are all generally of good height, of pleasing appearance and well built: I saw some who had indications of wounds on their bodies, and I asked them by signs if it was that, and they showed me that other people came there from other islands near by and wished to capture them and they defended themselves: and I believed and believe, that they come here from the continental land to take them captive. They must be good servants and intelligent, as I see that they very quickly say all that is said to them, and I believe that they would easily become Christians, as it appeared to me that they had no sect. If it please our Lord, at the time of my departure, I will take six of them from here to your Highnesses that they may learn to speak. I saw no beast of any kind except parrots on this island."

They very quickly say all that is said to them, and they will very easily become good slaves; good Christians also it appears, since the Admiral's research does not reveal the trace of any religious sect. And finally "I will take six of them"; ostensibly that they may learn to speak the language, but really that they may form the vanguard of cargo after cargo of slaves ravished from their happy islands of dreams and sunshine and plenty to learn the blessings of Christianity under the whip and the sword. It is all, alas, inevitable; was inevitable from the moment that the keel of Columbus's boat grated upon the shingle of Guanahani. The greater must prey upon the less, the stronger must absorb and dominate the weaker; and the happy gardens of the Golden Cyclades must be spoiled and wasted for the pleasure and enrichment of a corrupting civilisation. But while we recognise the inevitable, and enter into the joy and pride of Columbus and his followers on this first happy morning of their landing, we may give a moment's remembrance to the other side of the picture, and admit that for this generation of innocents the discovery that was to be all gain for the Old World was to be all loss to them. In the meantime, decrees the Admiral, they are to be freed and converted; and "I will take six of them that they may learn to speak."

There are no paths or footprints left in the sea, and the water furrowed on that morning more than four hundred years ago by the keels of Columbus's little fleet is as smooth and trackless as it was before they clove it. Yet if you approach Guanahani from the east during the hours of darkness you also will see a light that waxes and wanes on the horizon. What the light was that Columbus saw is not certain; it was probably the light from a torch held by some native woman from the door of her hut; but the light that you will see is from the lighthouse on Dixon Hill, where a tower of coral holds a lamp one hundred and sixty feet above the sea at the north-east point of the island. It was erected in no sentimental spirit, but for very practical purposes, and at a date when Watling's Island had not been identified with the Guanahani of Columbus's landfall; and yet of all the monuments that have been raised to him I can think of nothing more appropriate than this lonely tower that stands by day amid the bright sunshine in the track of the trade wind, and by night throws its powerful double flash every half-minute across the dark lonely sea. For it was by a light, although not of man's kindling, that Columbus was guided upon his lonely voyage and through his many difficulties; amid all his trials and disappointments, dimly as it must have burned sometimes, it never quite went out. Darkness was the name of the sea across which he took his way; darkness, from his religious point of view, was the state of the lands to which he journeyed; and, whatever its subsequent worth may have been, it was a burning fragment from the living torch of the Christian religion that he carried across the world with him, and by which he sought to kindle the fire of faith in the lands of his discovery. So that there is a profound symbolism in those raying beams that now, night after night, month by month, and year after year, shine out across the sea from Watling's Island in the direction of the Old World.

In the preparations for this voyage, and in the conduct and accomplishment of it, the personality of the man Columbus stands clearly revealed. He was seen at his best, as all men are who have a chance of doing the thing for which they are best fitted. The singleness of aim that can accomplish so much is made manifest in his dogged search for means with which to make his voyage; and his Italian quality of unscrupulousness in the means employed to attain a good end was exercised to the full. The, practical seaman in him carried him through the easiest part of his task, which was the actual sailing of his ships from Palos to Guanahani; Martin Alonso Pinzon could have done as much as that. But no Martin Alonso Pinzon or any other man of that time known to history had the necessary combination of defective and effective qualities that made Columbus, once he had conceived his glorious hazy idea, spend the best years of his life, first in acquiring the position that would make him listened to by people powerful enough to help him, and then in besieging them in the face of every rebuff and discouragement. Another man, proposing to venture across the unknown ocean to unknown lands, would have required a fleet for his conveyance, and an army for his protection; but Columbus asked for what he thought he had some chance of getting, and for the barest equipment that would carry him across the water. Another man would at least have had a bodyguard; but Columbus relied upon himself, and alone held his motley crew in the bonds of discipline. A Pinzon could have navigated the fleet from Palos to Guanahani; but only a Columbus, only a man burning with belief is himself and in his quest, could have kept that superstitious crowd of loafers and malefactors and gaol-birds to their duties, and bent them to his will. He was destined in after years for situations which were beyond his power to deal with, and for problems that were beyond his grasp; but here at least he was supreme, master of himself and of his material, and a ruler over circumstances. The supreme thing that he had professed to be able to do and which he had guaranteed to do was, in the sublime simplicity of his own phrase, "to discover new lands," and luck or no luck, help or hindrance, he did it at the very first attempt and in the space of thirty-five days. And although it was from the Pinta that the gun was fired, and the first loom of the actual land seen in the early morning, I am glad to think that, of all the number of eager watching men, it was Columbus who first saw the dim tossing light that told him his journey was at an end.

The End